The UnBecoming

A Collection of Poems by Shaill

MARIGOLD PRESS

Published in Savannah, Georgia by Marigold Press Books.

Marigold Press Books titles may be purchased in bulk for educational, business, fundraising, or sales promotional use. For information, please email marigoldpressbooks@gmail.com.

Author: Juneja, Shaillee
Title: The Unbecoming: A Collection of Poems by Shaill
ISBN: 979-8-9985495-8-8
Book and Cover Design: Russ Davis, Bravo Book Design
Photography: Valentina Portraiture

Printed in The United States of America

In Gratitude

~ ✦ ~

To those walking the path of unbecoming,
may these words be a lantern on your way home.

This book is dedicated to the man who gave me my first love – Words

Thank you Pitaji (grandfather), Amar Singh Chakkar, for instilling in
me the love of linguistics.

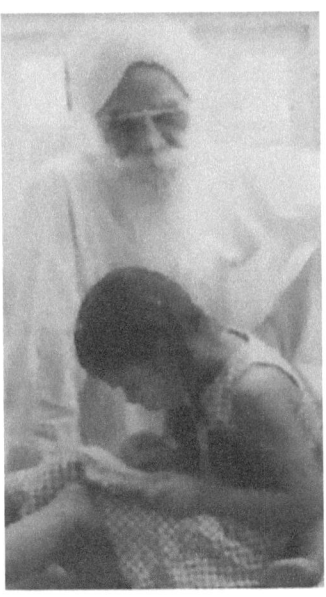

(Pitaji teaching me to write in multiple languages)

Foreword

~ ✦ ~

This collection was born not from a desire to write, but from a need to listen.

Each poem reflects the inner landscapes that go overlooked – the quiet corners of our truth, the restless dance of our ego, and the fleeting glimpses of stillness.

For much of my life, I wore layers of noise – the expectations of others, the conditioning of culture, the masks of survival. I confused those layers for my identity.

This collection are fragments of that unraveling – moments where I stumbled, resisted, surrendered, and slowly remembered. Each piece is less about reaching for something new and more about coming home to what was always here: my own unique light.

You will find the collection grouped into three phases of my journey – The Musings, The UnBecoming and lastly, Coming Home

I offer this collection not as a map, but as a lantern. May it remind you, too, that beneath the layers of doing, becoming, and performing, there is a self-untouched – your imperfectly perfect, luminous – whole.

In love and in light,
Shaill

Contents

Musings

~ ✦ ~

I made the leap

Leaving behind the life of chasing, outwardly successful but
unconscious living

I took a pause to hear the echoes of my inner self that kept tugging at
me

This was the beginning of my journey of just penning down what I
felt, observed and pondered on.

I did not have a purpose.

I did not have clarity or understanding why I had taken this detour.

But for once, I was willing to embrace the discomfort of not knowing
Next few writings are reflective of my emerging practice – pondering
and musing, albeit aimlessly, but still deeply

~ ✦ ~

Day 1: Kindness, Reverence and Perseverance in this Journey
Wed, 07 Mar 2012

We are taught to be brave – to face the adversities head on

We aspire to be super humans

Yet are we ignoring showering kindness to our humanness that what feels fear of rejection, of failure, that shies away from success for fear of our inadequacies

How can we be super humans if we cannot love our humanness

Sometimes we are so caught up in perfecting ourselves that we forget to see our beauty in as is.

I have embarked on this exciting journey of "the Next" in my life

Letting go is hard and full of excitement and then of some hurt – yet the journey is that of perseverance

Can I detach and make through this journey with dignity and grace

Can I believe that this journey is for a reason

Can I be kind to my own humanness

Can I keep the focus on abundance of future when faced with fear of passing of the present

~ ✦ ~

Satya and Satyavadi
Wed, 07 Mar 2012

Does Truth Always Need a Voice?

Does what is true always need a voice?
In service of Satya (truth),
must we become Satyavaadi –
those who proclaim it?

We see the world through our own lens –
colored by desertions, judgments, experience.
Even if the rules are set,
Is our truth the ultimate one?
And even if it is –
must it be spoken?

If it does not create wholeness,
if it only feeds Haume (ego),
What good does proclaiming bring?

Does truth always need a follower?
Or can Satya simply be,
whole and silent,
without a voice?

~ ✦ ~

The deafening noise of silence

Thu, 15 Mar 2012

As I stepped away from the chaos of being

I came to face with the deafening noise of silence

Who is it that I fear to find

Is it me or the nothingness

Be Still O silent one

Let me emerge

Let me embrace what I cannot deny

Be still

Mirror Mirror – Is that me?

Mon, 30 Apr 2012

A peek in the old mirror and we catch a glimpse of our changing reflection.

The surge of energy, the moments of doubts, being extremely uncomfortable in this new space of not knowing what the big grand plan is – but the serenity of putting together several small next steps.

When in years and years of working we start defining ourselves with what to do – it is very uncomfortable to come up with a quick introduction of self.

What that is time will unfold, and I am (getting) OK with not knowing :-) For now I look forward to 10 weeks of travel, exploration, photography, journaling and enjoying kids and family. Sometimes we have to step away from the life as we know it to start living again.

As she hugged me – She endearingly said – Ugh you even smell happy :D

In that moment I saw the longing of old me

Mirror mirror – was that me?

~ ~

Flowery linguistics too slow for email
Sun, 13 May 2012

For all the languish linguistics over text why mum over email.

Race to instant delivery and instant gratification seems to be one that is hard to keep up with

What happened to good ol' fashioned chewing on the words, penning them down and then the waiting for them to reach.

The patient anticipation of response seems to be absolved in this day and age.

Wonder how we will communicate with us 15 years from now

~ ~

Do I really create it?

Thu, 31 May 2012

The hard drilled lessons of . . ."I am the creator of my destiny" come to rigid contradiction with "God will not take you where his grace will not protect you"

So, do we really create our own destiny by asking the universe for what we want?

How do we know what we want is really the right thing for us?

And if it is not the right thing, then the universe will not grant it anyway . . .

So, then what is the point in answering – "Tum Chahte Kya ho?" (What do you want?)

~ ✦ ~

Careful! Spiritual Pride Ahead
Fri, 28 Aug 2015

When Ego Wears the Mask of Spirituality

We are all awakened to the desire for an inward journey in different ways. For some, it begins as a silent whisper within. For others, it's sparked by surroundings – or even dragged out of them by life itself.

Whatever the instigator, once we open ourselves to the blissful silence within, we are overcome with joy. Ecstatic. Grateful. Alive.

And then comes the urge to share that joy – or dare I admit to brag about my "advancement," my supposed accomplishment.

Recently, I faced this very dilemma. As a wannabe meditater, I've drifted in and out of phases where I felt deeply connected to higher energy. Yet there have also been stretches where I stacked excuse upon excuse:

"I don't believe in that form of meditation."

"My dharma is Karam Yog – I don't need to sit still."

"I'm too high-energy; I don't have the patience for it."

The truth is these are all defenses against deeper fears.

And yet, when I do succeed in surrendering and tasting bliss, my ego leaps in. It wants to measure my "progress," to label it, to share it. To wear a shiny new mask of being "spiritually elevated." But that, too, is just another dance of Maya.

Michael Singer writes in *The Surrender Experiment*:

"I didn't want to regain strength based on another mental concept of myself. Whenever I noticed thoughts being stitched together to create a new 'me,' I knocked the chair out from under them. It was painful, but I was willing to let it all go if it freed me to explore beyond."

His words echo my own realization: when I let ego define my spiritual experience, I step away from its purity. True presence is only felt in complete surrender – in being rooted in Now, not in analyzing the past or projecting onto the future.

Tibetan Buddhist teacher Chogyam Trungpa Rinpoche distilled it simply:

"Meditation is based on three fundamental factors – first, not centralizing inward; second, not longing to become higher; and third, becoming completely identified with the here and now."

What a humbling reminder. To notice the ego self as it tries to dance – and gently guide it back toward what matters: pure, unconditional surrender.

✧ May your day, too, be filled with bliss, wonder, and presence.

~ ✦ ~

Mirror Mirror – Who am I judging?

Sun, 30 Aug 2015

Often, our opinions are absolute.

Right and Wrong are markedly segregated.

We find ourselves surrounded by instigators of mental and verbal churn. People or situations continually invoke a response, an opinion within.

Even before dressing up that opinion with words (silent or out loud) to that opinion, we feel it within. It can be a warmth felt in our heart for joy, elation or a gut-wrenching feeling of disapproval or anger.

I cannot help but ponder – When we judge, who are we really judging? Where does that judgment stem from?

Why did we come across the circumstance that instigated the judgment

Our judgment is a physical manifestation of a deep-seated and an unresolved resistance within us

I recently heard the phrase "recycled ignorance."

It made me pause.

Yes, we all harbor (even the wisest ones amongst us) within us vast ignorance. And knowingly, unknowingly and at times begrudgingly (as social creatures of habit) we recycle our ignorance, again and again.

In an unconnected state, we are slaves to our addiction to continually recycle our ignorance. When instigated (i.e. interacting with a circumstance) we feel the uneasiness, the uprising of an opinion and an incessant need to label it, to declare it. to react to it and to stand by it.

We nourish the judgment with our mental chatter, our thoughts, our dialogue and our actions/reactions.

What if we committed ourselves to watching the judgment emerge, observing it, but not feeding it? What if we embraced the idea that every experience that invokes that strong felt resistance is a welcomed opportunity to create new experiences that will dissolve that fixed opinion – within the US.

So, when we are upset and in disagreement with someone/a circumstance – it is less about them but a WHOLE LOT about us.

For absolute truth does lie at the core of every occurrence. It is our journey to see it in varying shades of perspectives.

~ ✦ ~

We are all broken in our own unique ways.

Don't judge if light shines differently through their cracks.
Tue, 08 Sept 2015

Life is presenting us innumerable opportunities to Cleanse and
Evolve.

Disengage so you can acknowledge these teaching moments

Center yourself so you can sit with them and observe them happen

Open yourself so you can embrace them, can let 'em pass through

We are so caught up in fixing others that we miss the opportunity for
what we judge to Fix (Evolve) us.

Ironical indeed!

~ ✦ ~

Why need the spotlight when one has such radiance within

Thu, 22 Oct 2015

Such wisdom from Oh so Young

My son's latest creation "Immerse and Emerge" took my breath away this morning.

The haunting and transparent eyes are so captivating, they speak to you.

They invite you to Immerse in their hope and emerge radiant with life energy.

In my moment of parenthood pride, I wanted to share with all. I wanted him to submit the work for the school magazine.

And then he, in his grounded presence, looked at me and said, "Mom, one does not need to be in the limelight when one is comfortable in their space."

My hopeful (and self-absorbed) flight came to a screeching halt. I was dumbfounded.

True: Why need the Spotlight when one has such Radiance within. It is my "parental love and pride" for him or my own hidden narcissistic grandiosity.

For when fully grounded in abundance and inner radiance, we rarely need external validation.

Life brings about umpteen moments of awareness if we surrender ourselves to receive. So, here's a humble thanks to my lil' one for giving me an opportunity to climb down from my "parent pedestal" and bask in the abundant radiance that exists.

Yes – no spotlight needed here – For your inner light immerses this moment with truth and emerges as radiance that outshines all.

~ ✦ ~

My Kit Kat is not so special anymore (or is it?)

Sun, 21 Feb 2016

I was 10 when my father first brought me my first bag of Kit Kat chocolate. We lived in Delhi. His trips back from abroad were filled with stories of wonder and, of course, goodies.

It is not the first Barbie doll, or that motorized car that zipped through the floors of our living room, or that big fluffy teddy bear that seized the moment for me.

It was the first time I took a bite of that chocolate-covered wafer goodness. I vividly remember how the flavor exploded on my taste buds and how unreasonably obsessed and protective I became of that bag of chocolates – concocting plans to hide it from my siblings and hoping to make it last for a year till his next trip.

I would hide it in the deepest recesses of my closet. At night, dig out the molten mess and then tip toe into the kitchen to cool it in the freezer. I would then find a hidden corner and eat it in the silent dark solitude of the kitchen.

In years to come, receiving my new batch of Kit Kat supplies became the most anticipated outcome from my father's travels.

So, imagine my reaction when 7 years later I arrived in the U.S. for studies. I went to a gas station in New Jersey on the way to my university and saw bags and bags of Kit Kat chocolate being sold like common commodities along with several other brands of chocolates.

The goodness and the specialness were mass produced, and mass supplied. I felt such unexpected pang of disappointment.

My journey to discovering the spirit within has followed its own silent stubborn pace. I have been blessed to be surrounded by several family members who have been roaring down the path of spiritual growth and self-enlightenment for years.

I welcomed their guidance, listened and observed their journeys with wonder and, at times, envy. But as much as I intellectually understood the "Steps to mindfulness and connecting with the higher power within" my heart did not surrender to it.

Life continued to move at its pace. Filled with home, careers, young kids – my list of why I do not have time to meditate was long, fresh and always well fed. I do not know the exact moment when I surrendered and experienced God – but I have a feeling it was a few years ago during my nightly run.

I was lost in the rhythm of my breath and the sound of my feet hitting the concrete. In that silence, I inherently felt the need to shed off the cloaks of "my thinking," my active mind, my ego.

In those brief moments of nothingness, I felt immeasurable abundance. A kind of love that runs so deep and is so profound that you cannot describe it in words. Because no words or worldly description can do justice to the purity and the lightness of that moment. I felt as if a door was opened within me. I had discovered this secret entrance to a place of abundance.

Ironically, the pathway to this place of truth and wonder was opposite to what my active mind was trained to do.

The secret lied in the surrender to the pause – fully and wholesomely being with the pause. In that moment I felt this connection to a light and energy that exists within me.

As if a book was being read to me or I was reading it – because it was my own voice in my being, except that words did not have any decibel energy to them. They emerged and were present in my consciousness.

I suddenly believed in God, undoubtedly experiencing his presence in every fiber of my being. I experienced Me and I was an extension of God. It is not a chase to God, but a surrender and inward journey to what lies within.

My "mindfulness practice" looks like a secret life of its own. It emerged in midst of utmost levels of physical activity – when I was on my runs, running races, in the midst of chaos in my day-to-day life.

I often doubted – Could the truth be really so Uncomplicated, Unglamorous and Drama Free? Was the pathway to simply surrendering to nothingness to experience the utmost abundance?

Surely, I have it wrong because I am not slogging through the complexities of spiritual wisdom and living through the trials and tribulations of spiritual growth.

I am attending my very first wisdom conference this year. In many ways I feel like a fish from a small pond in the midst of a crowd of a large ocean. The last 24 hours have been awe filled. I have felt inspired, overwhelmed and jaded.

Spirituality has been a deeply personal and private experience to me. I can tap into that space when I shed away the Me and My wisdom.

However, towards the end of the day, as I stood still in the midst of the moving crowd, familiar feelings surfaced within me from the past.

It felt like the goodness and specialness is being mass produced, and mass supplied.

It is being packaged into many brands and commoditized.

My Kit Kat does not feel so special anymore.

Or perhaps it still is, and I must uncover its specialness all over again.

Serendipitous – I think not!

Mon, 22 Feb 2016

At times our silent intentions surface as chance encounters.

Ones that clear up the mirk and turn your attention to what is hidden deep inside dark, fearful, abandoned alleys of your psyche.

Today I met two such angels who nudged me just enough to see what was hiding behind the complacency and contentment.

Serendipitous – I think not!

For we attract from the universe what we need most.

And it brought me these two warm, gregarious and gracious angels. Sometimes the inspiration we seek from outside lies beneath tangled ties within.

Serendipitous – I – think – not!

~ ~

The Tug between the Cs
Wed, 24 Feb 2016

The dark abandoned galley ways of our psyche are fascinating places to wander into.

At times we find answers to questions we have been mulling over and sometimes we uncover the mirk that makes us pause even further.

When attempting to practice stillness within the constant flow of life, at times, we wonder if we are being Content or Complacent.

Each seems to somewhat co-exist alongside the other and we ebb and flow out of them throughout our journey. I do not believe in grandiosity of one over another for Shadow is just another form of existence as the Light. The key differential is which way does our inner light shine on to.

When we are operating out of a space of faith in the universe, in our being, we can take on any action (pursuit of a goal) or an action (resisting the urge to pursue more) with contentment.

When we pursue a misguided action (a compromise) or an inaction (not choosing to pursue an action) we are operating from a place of cynicism, fear of failure and judgment. We are being complacent.

As such, both states of Contentment and Complacency can equally guide us to an action or an inaction.

Contentment can often be misjudged as Complacency when we practice stillness.

Our potential for growth is beyond the single dimensional measure of worldly achievements. Our true potential is immeasurable and can support multi-faceted pursuits.

However, key to all pursuits is stillness – wholesome and complete surrender to the present moment.

So, when in the midst of the tugs of two Cs – Take a pause and commit to the present moment with pure intent.

As my wise fellow yogini says, " When Soul consciousness is active, stillness speaks.

Stillness speaks and honors the motion of life.

Soul can create good fortune by sharing love and pure intent."

Here's to creating a loving reminder to trust the flow of the universe!

~ ~

Stillness

Wed, 02 Nov 2016

The abundance that rests in stillness

The strength realized in surrender

The possibilities that emerge in restraint

For right at the heart of life's paradoxes

Lies our absolute truth

Can you see

Wed, 02 Nov 2016

in the midst
is the silent roar
buried deep within
is the escape
Can you see?

~ ✦ ~

I-am-searching
Fri, 11 Nov 2016

I am not angry

I am not disappointed

There is an emptiness I feel

A numb emptiness that engulfs me within

This choice was not about him

This choice was not about what he would do for us

This choice was about who we are, in our hearts, in our soul

And I naively believed past the musk of negative rhetoric

We have more goodness, more integrity

~ ✦ ~

Detangle

Tue, 29 Nov 2016

sometimes you must take

a peek from above to detangle

from all that weighs you down

and

see the beauty that is

~ ✦ ~

The UnBecoming

~ ✦ ~

When the silent echoes of my musings became deafening
My ego's resistance began to wane

I gave in
My Unraveling began

~ ✦ ~

Latching on, so very hard

Tue, 13 Dec 2016

To our expectations

Why so?

What do we fear?

What is that anger and that resentment really towards?

Our expectations are our inner resistance and fear of as-is

A fear and a judgment that we feed with inner chatter – consistently

We put the burden of expectations of change on others so that

We can misplace the true responsibility of self-assurance

For if we are not complete on our own,

how can we be complete with others

Let us, detangle,

Be free and let others Be Free

We are each on a journey to live our unique truths, embrace our darkness and accept ourselves as a whole.

Let Go

Live More

Be Free

~ ✦ ~

In the hustle to Become

Sun, 14 May 2017

In the hustle to Become,

We neglect to Be.

In the glorious pursuit of mountaintops,

We overlook the abundance that exists in the valleys.

For in these troughs

We Unlearn and we Unbecome.

We see the glory and grandeur of As-Is

And we are Enough

~ ✦ ~

Muted

Sat, 10 Jun 2017

Pain muted

Under the burden of obligations

Turns into a deafening roar that rips through the being.

Yearn to be free in the unfree world

Jaded by the caring wisdom it offers.

Unshackle

Let go

Turn within to be without.

~ ✦ ~

Ruminate
Fri, 16 Jun 2017

The incessant need
To Ruminate
To assess
To judge
To label
To box
To leverage
To fix
For it forges a path of avoidance
From as-is
From Now
The incessant need
To over do
To impress
To prove
To be bigger than self
To be grander than as-is
To be apart
Draining
Depleting
Exhausting.
Pause to Be
To be with as-is
To be with as-is in Now
Unlearn to ruminate
Be free.

~ ✦ ~

Unravel

Mon, 17 Jul 2017

Unfold

Unwind

Unravel

Fall apart

Can you see

Can you embrace

Scattered

Broken

Cracked

Can you let the light shine through

In the imperfect perfection of you

Can you bask in the splendor

Can you unbecome to become

Can you?

The incessant need to be
Fri, 21 Jul 2017

Bigger than ourselves

As if then we will be enough.

What if we already are enough

Grander than enough

For the journey is not outward and upward

But inward and be still

In the service of as is

We uncover

What is

~ ✦ ~

Resilience

Fri, 04 Aug 2017

I wasn't sure you would

But you did

The soil was not right

The pot was too tight

The sun was ruthless

You wilted,

you lay low,

you stayed still

And then you bloomed

~ ~

All those words
Fri, 11 Aug 2017

With silence in between

Deep in that deafening roar of silence

Lies the paradoxical truth of us

So, give me those silent words

Give me that silent pause

Give me the absolute

~ ✦ ~

Unveil

Thu, 31 Aug 2017

I walked in

Expecting to be broken

to be shattered apart

so, I could Unravel.

Instead found you,

The silent stubborn strength

basking at the brinks of resilience.

I went in searching for the silent roar,

You were always by my side.

Reaching out, emerging,

waiting to be seen.

Can you see me?

I do

I do see you

I do hear you

The Light Within

~ ✦ ~

Are you?

Wed, 06 Sept 2017

Light and shadows

So intricately intertwined in fabric of my being

Can you see?

It asked

Do you want to unveil?

For the question is not if it is listening

Rather if you are ready to

Ah the paradoxes that guard the absolute

~ ✦ ~

Can you see?

Tue, 12 Sept 2017

Mirror mirror what do u see.

Is it me?

Can you see??

And then it said – for the question is not Can I see.

The Question is Are You Willing to See.

Are You Willing to Hear

For choose we must
Sun, 01 Oct 2017

This path of letting go

Of unraveling

Of falling apart

Of being scattered, messy and afraid.

So, we could unveil

That which is

Which is our absolute.

So that we could hear that silent roar within

That speaks our gloriously imperfect truth.

We are already that we seek.

And the journey is not to transcend outwards and upwards but inward and within. Ah Love!

~ ~

A life in progress
Fri, 13 Oct 2017

Unraveling

Unveiling

And then basking in the glory of all that

Imperfect perfection of self

~ ✦ ~

Ah that space
Sat, 21 Oct 2017

That opens when we let go

All that was too costly to hold on to.

Space to be treaded upon with an open heart and a bared soul.

Breath that fills you up with light and hope.

Faith renewed with an empowered perspective of your love.

Humbled.

~ ✦ ~

Finding

Mon, 23 Oct 2017

Finding

Dignity and grace

in the perfectly imperfect essence of self

Oh, this searching

This yearning.

~ ✦ ~

Coming Home

~ ✦ ~

In the throes of falling apart,
In the death of my old self,
I stubbornly, and at times, desperately held on
I held on to the belief that I will birth anew.

And I did
I came home to Me

~ ✦ ~

Soulful defiance

Tue, 31 Oct 2017

of living
To be birthed anew
Alive with that light
That makes us see
the glorious loving of as-is
That is Fiery Perseverance

What I know for sure is
Sun, 18 Feb 2018

That I am love and love is in me

That my journey is to be love and bask in that surrender

That as I shed, I rise

Rise to be what I am destined to be

That as I crack, I Luminate

Luminate the light that fills me

That as I embrace

I become whole

Whole with his divinity

That in this love lies my unbreakable courage

Courage to be, courage to give, courage to receive

What I know for sure is

That I am love and love is in me

~ ✦ ~

Be seen

Thu, 22 Mar 2018

Embracing

Accepting

the messy humanness of being.

Freedom

Light in vulnerability of self.

Shedding

Soaring

Reveling

in the glorious imperfections.

Loving

Caring for the self

Courage in seen with as-is

What a journey!

Let go of that hustle

Thu, 29 Mar 2018

Hustle ,Hustle, Hustle

For more

For that chase

For that space

Give more, more, more

Take less

Dim that spark

Think, worry, ponder

Take a Pause

Own your space

Be still

Feet firmly planted, stand tall

Heart full, grateful

Trust and Shine On.

~ ✦ ~

Practicing Compassion towards our Judgment

Fri, 30 Mar 2018

Our opinions are absolute.

Our sense of right and wrong are so markedly segregated.

People and situations invoke a response within us and even before we have dressed up our response in words, we can feel it deep within us.

It can be a feeling of joy or elation or a gut-wrenching feeling of anger, disappointment or resentment. As we nourish this judgment with our thoughts, our words, our actions and our reactions, it grows stronger and becomes an absolute for us.

We find ourselves transitioning from judgment to anger, and from anger to contempt.

At times I cannot help but wonder – What is the root of this judgment? What evokes these feelings within us? And how can we control it?

One morning, in the quiet of nature, something occurred to me: What if we are what we roaringly and unapologetically judge?

Maybe what creates this deep rooted and charged response within us is our own shadow, our own unresolved beliefs and experiences.

This realization was very unsettling.

I realized that most of my judgments assumed me as being on a higher pedestal of morality, character traits and values. My judgments were justified as reactions to bad behaviors and flawed morality of those I judged.

The urge to prove my righteous point of view was often strong and it caused me to latch on to my judgments, hold back on empathy and forgiveness.

For how I could forgive and embrace those who devalue others? My own contempt was easily justified in my head.

In the end, I was invariably being what I so vehemently judged in others.

49

I paused.

The realization was also humbling. I recognized that I needed to strip myself of my own self-righteousness.

Despite differing value systems and beliefs, we all share a single humanity. And suffering is common to all of humanity. And for those who, in my mind, propagate the suffering with their words or actions, I struggle practicing compassion.

I turned to my friends and mentors.

I had long, heart-felt conversations with middle and high schoolers with whom I work. I recognized that the root of all judgments lies within our own vulnerabilities and our deep-rooted fears and insecurities.

Understanding this suffering allows us to adopt a mindful view of circumstances we are judging. A compassionate outlook does not mean we are accepting the angry and contentious behavior of others. In fact, it allows us to practice mindfulness in simply observing what is the motivation behind those in distress and anger and prompting them to make their choices.

It allows interactions to be potentially fruitful.

At minimum, it allows for a diffusion of power of judgments and unrest within us so we are more grounded – and ultimately, our end goal should be our OWN growth.

When we practice compassion towards our judgment, we are in turn being kind and empathetic to our own inner selves.

We subdue the feeling of powerlessness or the urge to establish our righteousness.

It feels like a tall order most days, but most empowering when one can do it. When we compassionately embrace the thinking behind what we judge, we feel whole.

And when we feel whole, we are closer to the goodness within us.

~ ✦ ~

See through

Sat, 31 Mar 2018

When that extraordinary lurks behind the seemingly ordinary

It makes it seem off.

But that it the cue

To see through

To see beyond

To see past the distraction of that broken ordinary

When has the lotus blossomed in the clear clean

It's the extraordinariness of that mud and mirk

That nurtured the pristine

~ ✦ ~

This

Fri, 06 Apr 2018

This fire within

This rising within

To be more than what is

To be grander than what is

What does it feed on

What does it live off

What does it run away from

When does it stay put

And see what is

Embrace what is

Bask in what is

To strip off that cloak

And be seen

To find that courage and stay with It over and over again

Ah the messy business of our humanness

~ ✦ ~

Write

Fri, 20 Apr 2018

Cause that need

To explore

Experience

Express

To unravel

Unlearn

To Reveal

Revel

To hear

Feel

Fear

To embrace

And be alive

Write Not to know

But to figure it out

Write Not for those wants

But for those needs

~ ~

In balance
Fri, 20 Apr 2018

We ought to be

Do we know?

To not pour but cry

To not soar but smile

To not roar but resent

To not shatter but grieve

To not soar but stand

To not spread those wings and fly

To not fall but stay put

In balance

We ought to be

Do we know?

~ ✦ ~

Father

Fri, 20 Apr 2018

I come from the same aching blood.

Desperate for attention and consumed by dreams.

I crumble, falter, fall.

Fire in my belly and restless ambition in my veins.

I leap with all that faith

That I am your daughter.

You and I

Thu, 10 May 2018

Through my feet

Into her belly

We are connected

You and I

Through my heart

Into your soul

We are connected

You and I

Through my soaring Into your grounding

We are connected

You and I

Through my pain Into your hurt

We are connected

You and I

Where I end You begin

You and I

We are connected.

Your music

Sun, 20 May 2018

Who you are deep within
What your music is
To hum that tune
To follow that music
To be that . . . unapologetically
Is the gift of aging

~ ~

I too am

Fri, 08 Jun 2018

I too am a daughter who learned that her daddy wanted to die.

He fought hard through the deep dark blues just as I have fought myself.

I too am a mom who works so hard, some days, to keep it together and have a happy and a strong front for whom I love.

I too am a friend who hides those blues in a deep dark closet painted on the outside with cheerful murals, too embarrassed to show it all.

I too am that coworker – competent and passionate, bringing her whole to her commitments, even on days when it is too big a burden to carry.

But I am also that strong woman who is not afraid to speak up against this stigma.

And lend a hand, reach out to those who grapple with these blues.

#MentalIllness is real, it's tangible and deserves the same openness and advocacy as any other physical illness. It is a rising epidemic in our society and amongst us all.

Stand up to this stigma. Educate yourself. Help create resources for those in need. And fight for those who struggle with it . . . even if it is a fight for one.

~ ✦ ~

Oh yes, we are
Sat, 14 Jul 2018

Oh yes, we are

Evolving that is

The kind that makes us Go inward

To that light that shines within

To that abundance of nothingness

To that deafening roar of our silence.

Oh yes, we are Evolving that is

Reclaiming our light

When our shadows seem the darkest.

Oh yes, we are Embracing

The luminous

The divine

The unbreakable

The unlimited Love – that is us.

Oh. Yes. We. Are.

~ ✦ ~

Would you?

Sat, 28 Jul 2018

Would you

With fire in your soul

And grace in your heart

Take that leap?

Beyond all that is known

Is safe

Is accepted

Would you

Tread that path . . . alone?

Would you hold courage

with fear

Humility

with confidence

Confusion

with surety

And hold it all while letting go?

Could you?

Fiery perseverance to be

Sat, 28 Jul 2018

Fiery perseverance to be

Unapologetically

Unabashedly

Your own light

Your own music

Fiery perseverance to be

To transform

To blossom

To be the lotus

Fiery perseverance to become – "tapass"

~ ~

Resilience
Wed, 08 Aug 2018

Get up

Dust off

Pursue

Persist

Again and again

Refuel

Go within

Tap into that fire

Gather these pieces

Outshine those cracks

Wear them proud

Head held high

Heart filled with grace

Go at it again

That is Resilience

In between Being and Becoming

Wed, 15 Aug 2018

In that place of unknown

When you have walked away from what was

Determined to Become

Yet waiting for the path to unveil

In that place of pause

In the midst of trough

Waiting to ride to the ebb

Looking up, looking beyond

At the horizon

Hopeful and determined

In that place of surrender

Unraveling and Unveiling

Reveling in faith

In the glory of what is within

The fire in the soul

The grace in the heart

In that place in between

That hopeful, pregnant pause

~ ✦ ~

Fearfully courageous

Thu, 16 Aug 2018

Fearfully courageous

Doubtful

but oh, so sure

Cautious but ready to leap

With shaky stubborn determination

Going at it scared – that's courage

Fearful yet courageous

~ ✦ ~

Belonging
Thu, 16 Aug 2018

Are you standing where you belong?

Are you safe

Protected

Unhurt?

Are you tearing apart that refuge?

Oh Darlin'

For if you have not fallen apart

Failed spectacularly

Hurt miserably

You have not lived

You have not learned

You have not come alive.

To live or to be alive

For choose we must.

Mumblings
Fri, 17 Aug 2018

Am I too much

Am I taking too much space

Am I too self-promoting

Should I dim it out a little

What would they think

What would they critique

What if they write it off

What if nothing comes out of it

What if it is all in vain

All that holds you down

Shackles you in that box

Of safe

Known

Acceptable

And Appropriate

What would you do with them mumblings?

For he was his father's son
Thu, 06 Sept 2018

And I am his daughter

That restless ambition

That love for words

That aching blood, desperate for attention and consumed by dreams

Hungry for love,

for belonging,

for creating

Crumbling Faltering Falling

And leaping up again and again

For he was his father's son.

He succumbed to his fire

And I am his daughter . . . I see it too

Walking the path
Thu, 15 Nov 2018

In between Being and Becoming

I keep unraveling

I keep unveiling what's within

The glory of faith,

of your love

Am I willing to see, you asked?

I am

I embrace, dear lord

I give in and surrender to your will

Fearfully courageous

I commit to purity

Purity of intentions

Purity of service

With fire in my belly and grace in my heart

I surrender to your will

to create,

to be the voice,

to elevate.

I walk the path with grace

In between Being and Becoming.

~ ✦ ~

Oh Yes You Must!

Thu, 15 Nov 2018

Lost in that pursuit

Engulfed in that persistence

Determined to create

She asked, "Should I?"

He said, "Oh yes – you must,

It's your right,

It's your voice"

And then she knew

She would

She could

She will

~ ✦ ~

Still

Fri, 16 Nov 2018

"You are stillness"

She spoke

So how can you be carried away

Be you

Be Here

Be Now

Fear is an internal story

A story that ego creates

So, it can exist

Don't resist,

Rest, Be Still

Let creation Flow

You are stillness

So how can you be carried away

~ ~

My voice

Mon, 07 Jan 2019

It waivers

Is shy and unsure

Is mine

It comes from deep depths

From dark crevices

Where Hope seeps in

It comes from the cracks

From when I broke apart

And was put together anew

It comes from that raw shiny surface

Scrubbed clean from having shed those layers

My voice

Comes from the depth of my being

From my ego

From my soul

From my light

My Voice Gives me hope

Gives me purpose

What's yours?

~ ✦ ~

Journey of a passionate innovator
Sat, 12 Jan 2019

Openness to be misunderstood

Humility to self-reflect

Conviction to believe in your vision

And discipline to incrementally push through

And wine 😊

~ ✦ ~

Being

Sun, 27 Jan 2019

I pondered

I searched

I asked

Only to unveil

That I was already

What I wanted to become

Gloriously divine

Unabashedly Human

Relentlessly committed

To awaken

To blossom

To become

"What does it matter" it said

The façade of perfection

Of exploration

For the absolute truth

Needs no explanation

No validation

No phosphatized unveiling

It is subtle

It is profound

It is knowing of what is

I hustled

I hustled

I hustled

To become

Only to fall on my knees

And Embrace Being

~ ✦ ~

What would a dude do?

Thu, 07 Feb 2019 01:46:14 +0000

WHAT WOULD A DUDE DO?

Recently I came to a crossroads on a professional decision. I was chatting with a good friend of mine, more like venting and debating my options concerns, insecurities and all that could be a barrier to success.

She listened to me patiently and then said,

What would a dude do?

Interestingly, I immediately switched modes and spurted out logical steps to assessment and decision making for the opportunity. It was clear, concise and action driven. It made me pause –

What a contrast between the masculine and feminine energy that I carry . . . AND what made me mark each of those perspectives with those labels?

I had been stewing during a walk with my kiddo. And he made a good observation . . . There is so much media focus on women empowerment, the rise of feminine energy. Isn't equality about the ability to tap into both masculine and feminine energy that we all have within?

For one is not better than the other and both together make wisdom and true empowerment. Ladies, love your inner dude as much as your badass feminine selves.

And I gotta give some love to my lil' wise one

~ ✦ ~

Will they?

Tue, 12 Feb 2019

Will these wings take me

To the depths of my being

Behind those shadows

Deep in the dark crevices where my light hides

Will they?

Will they take me soaring beneath the abyss

Where nothing remains

But the deafening roar of silence that hums my truth

Will they?

Will they take me to the unison with my gloriously divine self

That lovingly graces and embraces this form

Like a queen perched on her throne radiating, immersing and
emerging

Fulfilling her purpose, her destiny to become what she yearns to be
Will they?

Will they take me to the oneness with the infinity that is my
forgotten home

Will these wings take me to those forgotten depths?

~ ✦ ~

What if ?!?

Mon, 18 Feb 2019

This illusion of separation From the divine

This aspiration to become worthy of His grace

This burden of our imperfect selves

Carrying the burden of karmic cycles

It couldn't be!

What if we already are

What we aspire to become

What if we are HIM in our existence

What if the journey is not to become worthy of divine love but to be the glorious divinity we are

What if all of this illusion of separation of unworthiness is a sham to be broken through

What if that path of lonely belief is to be treaded alone

What if the answer is to break away from the known paradigm of HIM and follow the unknown but unshakable hunch

Ah crud's this bidness of awakening!! It was to bring clarity and peace. eh?

What if instead it breaks everything apart in chaos and shambles

~ ✦ ~

Why must we?

Tue, 26 Feb 2019

Why must we?

Be swallowed by darkness to know the light

Be consumed by pain to know the pleasure

Be broken apart by deceit to know the love

Why must we experience the polarity to appreciate the absolute

An excuse to cover up for the fallacies, is it?

if we are that love and light, why must we become worthy of that
oneness that we are

Only to start that chase all over again

Why must we?

~ ~

My Freedom

Tue, 05 Mar 2019

Cloaked as loss of hope

With silent footsteps

It roared in my being

Weaved tightly in my compulsions

In my aversions

In my expectations

It kept drowning

Buried under my charred remains

My freedom raised itself from my crumbled ashes.

She silently stood in my heart

And whispered – 'Tis You, Only You who completes Thyself

My freedom It roared in my being

And left me yearningly complete.

~ ✦ ~

That space

Thu, 07 Mar 2019

In that space between knowing and being

Vulnerable

Unsure

Stripped Naked and raw

In that space between ego and spirit

Unrealized

Unawakened

Foolishly wise

In that space between becoming and being

Yearning for the nectar of divine

The oneness

The stillness

The steadiness

The wholeness

In that space being knowing and being,

I search for my stillness so elusively within

So impossibly close

Must I travel to depths of darkness to shine the light?

How else could the light become its shine unless deeply intertwined
and in love with the darkness

Embrace that darkness with fierce compassion, with abandon

And the light shines brighter.

In the journey between knowing and being I face myself over and
over again

~ ✦ ~

You, my love

Fri, 15 Mar 2019

You, my love,

the stubborn will to survive

To thrive

To overcome

To embrace

To become

You, my love, the stubborn will to survive

Your fall on your knees

You crumble

Only to rise up again

Luminating through the cracks

You radiate your stubborn charm

You, my love, my stubborn will to survive

You are too stubborn to stay down.

~ ✦ ~

Allow

Tue, 14 May 2019

Allow

This word . . .

The insurmountable strength

and unreachable depth in it

To align and allow

To surrender and allow

To love, to forgive and allow

To Be and Allow

The divine will to dance through the essence . . .

Is the dance to be allowed

Allow it

~ ✦ ~

Discernment

Sun, 19 May 2019

Discernment on the path of service – what is in service to the light within and what is feeding my ego!

"Nishkaam Seva" (ego-less service)

Going inwards.

Cleansing, shedding the layers.

For it is easy to assume an identity of "service" to fill the voids within.

~ ~

What does it look like?
Wed, 05 Jun 2019

I have been speaking with warriors of HOPE, champions of mental health across the globe for the past few weeks. With program leads for UNICEF, United Nations, World Health Organization in war torn regions; with leads of mental health programs at home NAMI Texas and with people like you and me who cope with it.

It has been humbling to reflect upon the colors it gets painted in, the lens through which we see mental health globally and how the common thread weaves through it all – need for acceptance, for education, for destigmatization and for compassion

The face of mental illness, what does it look like?

a high functioning alcoholic

an anxious teen

a successful narcissist

a vulnerable artist

a grieving parent

a closeted sexuality

a high-flying corporate executive

an exuberant friend – deceptive, wide eyed, hiding behind expressions, it is adept at escaping.

The face of mental illness, what does it look like?

Vulnerable

Strong

Beautiful

Broken

Resilient

Scared

It is adept at hiding behind normalcy.

The face of mental illness, what does it look like?

Vacant eyes

Broken bodies

Emptied hearts

Crying souls

It hides under survival.

The face of mental illness, what does it look like?

Like you

Like me

Like one next to us, here and there

It is all of us.

Then why do we look to paint it differently than us.

Them, Those people, each one of them.

The face of mental illness – it's me, it's you.

~ ✦ ~

Anew

Fri, 27 Dec 2019

As it bades goodbye, the year 2019, I sit in silence reminiscing all that it brought

Learnings

Unlearnings

And the Unveilings.

Laughter joy Success

And the Growth.

It is said, when you embrace your truth, you step into the portal of your soul

Your story, your history, your victories and your mistakes all are in divine order for they are all opportunities to step into your destiny.

When and how you choose to step in, is your free will – it is your journey.

At the threshold of the new decade, I stand cracked open and raw, baring my all. Grieving what I am leaving behind

And trusting the path ahead, the voice within.

I surrender to be birthed anew

Anew into Hope,

Into purpose

Into trust, love and faith

Forgiving self and them I shed the grudges and the judges and the doubting

Filled with His Love and light,

I surrender to faith

in His Grace

~ ✦ ~

I may not

Tue, 21 Jan 2020

I may not see the way ahead

But I am not lost

To shed the as-is

To be engulfed

in quietness,

in loneliness,

in solitude

Was to be done to hear your humming

I may not see the way ahead

But I know it's there

The path ahead of newness

Of realignment

I may not see the way ahead

But I know you surround me

Leading the way within

I may not see the way ahead

But I hear you deep within

Teaching me to see the light

To trust the knowingness

How could I be lost

when each moment in this abyss Is in search of Me

I may not see the way ahead

But I am loving losing myself

to find Me

~ ✦ ~

. . . but I AM

Sun, 02 Feb 2020

but I AM

I might not be fearless

but I AM COURAGE

courage to take my chance

to pursue the possibilities

I might not be fearless, but I AM BELIEVER

believer in the divine will

I might not be fearless, but I AM RESPECTFUL

Respectful of my boundaries and essence

I might not be fearless

but I AM ABUNDANT

abundantly entrenched in his love and light

I might not be fearless

but I AM WILLING and ABLE

to create synergy with my soul's calling

~ ✦ ~

You are Whole
Thu, 06 Feb 2020

You are

You are whole, even in your brokenness

You see, my love,

how could you not be

You are his spirit,

his love and his light

What feels, what looks like lack is his impetus for you to soar

to fill your soul with experiences you call for

My love, you are whole and abundant

So go on, show up and claim your glorious light

~ ✦ ~

I don't want to win, I want life (w/ translation)
Tue, 21 Jul 2020

"Jeetna nahin Jeena hai

Mujhe Khushi se

Apni soch se

Apne guroor se

Bas ~ ab aur nahin

Aur nahin yeh ziddo zehed

Lene ki

Paane ki

Cheenne ki

Batane ki

Sunne ki

Sunaane ki

Han yeh sach hai

Aise hi hota hai

Aise hi chalti hai duniya

Aise hi nibhate hain aur torre jatein hai rishte

Lekin ab banaana hai khud se rishta

In awaazon se door

Apne suroor pe

Jeetna nahin jeena hai mujhe"

LOOSELY TRANSLATED.

I don't want the win,

I want to live

In happiness

Humming my own music

Living my integrity

No more,

anymore

of this hustle

To take

To possess

To listen

To tell

Yes, it's true

The world does this dance

This is how relationships are Lived And broken apart

It's time For that relationship within

away from the noise

Humming to that music, within

I don't want the win, I want life

~ ✦ ~

The conundrum of stillness

Tue, 01 Sept 2020

In that emptiness

In that abyss – is the beginning

Yet we spend lifetimes in motion

Chasing stillness

In that void, the darkness – its finally seen

Yet we spend lifetimes chasing light

In the letting go is the unison

Yet we spend lifetimes chasing possession

The conundrum of stillness

It resides in at the heart of chaos, in the throes of falling apart

~ ✦ ~

I see you
Tue, 01 Sept 2020

I see you

I do

I see the dichotomy you lived

To be strong, independent, smart

Yet not too much

For being subservient is sanskaari (cultured)

To be vocal, articulate, righteous

Yet not too much

For being tolerant is samajhdaar (wise)

To put on a strong, happy front

While being broken

For being silent is sehensheel (tolerant)

I see you love

I do

I see the pain you disregarded

Under the disguise of self-growth

Under the burden of Karma

I see your sunshine

I do

I practiced disregard of your inner voice

As it was the weakness that must be overcome

The practiced dimming of your shine

As you must not outshine others

The practiced acceptance-of as-is

As you must comply with fears that were not even yours

I also see you my love

As you detach yourself

from the suffering

This contrast

For All as brought you to Now

So, you can choose

the vibration of

The love within

The light within

I see you love

I do

All of you

And you are luminous

~ ~

Listening

Sun, 06 Sept 2020

Listening to the pain

Of those that have given hurt

Is not often easy

But is the path of choice

There is a luminosity in the midst of all that connects us

We are all but stories

Even the dark ones

Intertwined

Interconnected

Inter dependent

Ebbing and flowing through light and darkness

Ebbing and flowing and dancing to our music

Ebbing and flowing and living our stories

Light and dark

Giving and taking

Pain and happiness

Is all but expression of those stories

Can you see?

Can you hear?

~ ✦ ~

She soared
Mon, 21 Sept 2020

She soared

From under the voiceless cloak

Of burdens

Of expectations

Of fear

She peeked

And heard the hum of her soul

You my love are gloriously whole

Gloriously whole in your brokenness

You my love have waited long

Waited long to sing out aloud

Your song

And now

Its time

Its time

To Let go

To pull apart

To fall apart

And come together anew

Anew in your essence

She simmered in the knowing of it all

She gathered her broken wings

Feather by feather

She summoned

Those that watched over her silently

And then

She Rose

She rose from the ashes of her as-is

And soared

To the possibilities of what would be

She soared

Singing the song of her soul

Becoming all, she would be

Never looking back

She soared

~ ✦ ~

Wisdom . . . is it?

Sat, 26 Sept 2020 18:26:29 +0000

Wisdom . . . is it?

To allow,

embrace,

accept

In the name of keeping peace

To put away

Your voice

Your boundaries

In the name of keeping, it intact

Why do we become this

Voiceless

Powerless

But wise and a good girl

Why do we choose Their voice over our music

Why do we forget who we are

Why do we give in

Wisdom in tradition . . . is it?

Wholeness in Brokenness
Mon, 05 Oct 2020

Feeling broken, I lie curled up on the floor, wallowing in pain and self-pity.

I had failed at that pursuit or perfection, that perceived wholesome that I chased for long.

I looked at the scattered pieces of my being, and wondered if I could ever be whole again: How do I show up in life with my brokenness?

I realized, ironically, the only way to heal the pain is to fully embrace it. Go through the darkness. Sit with that void, that hurts. Resist the urge to push it away, fill it up with noise, distractions and activities.

When we become still and one with our pain, we can see what is hidden underneath it. Our subconscious beliefs. For me, I saw that my life, my choices were manifestations of my subconscious beliefs.

I placed my sense of duty, my fear of rejection, my need for acceptance and approval above my sense of dignity. I drowned my inner voice of truth with outer chatter or validations.

And yes, it was tempting to fill my heart with anger, rejection and blame but to what avail. The only path to redemption is love. His love, self-love. So, I worked on forgiveness. Forgiveness of others.

When hurt, anger, blame would raise its roar, I would acknowledge it, embrace it and then let it pass though. I would replace them with prayers of love and light.

I worked even harder to forgive myself (and that is an ongoing journey). Forgive myself for falling short, for falling apart, for giving in, for not choosing the truth. I learned to see the hidden radiance in my shadows. For they are nothing but opportunities of growth.

I learned to see beauty in my broken self, my cracks.

Oh yes, His light pours through those cracks in me. So, when I ponder, how do I show up with my brokenness? Could I ever be whole again?

The answer comes roaring in my being – You are whole already, even in your brokenness

My Love, You Are!

You are whole, even in your brokenness.

You see, how could you not be?

You are His spirit, His love and His light.

What feels like, what looks like lack is His impetus for you to soar,

To fill your soul with experiences you call for.

My love, you are whole.

So, go on, show up and claim your glorious light!

Experience the richness of setbacks and leapfrog into your journey.

For you are gloriously whole, even in your brokenness.

~ ✦ ~

Broken, but whole

Fri, 23 Oct 2020

Broken, but whole
Beaten but not wounded
Parched but not thirsty
Wounded but not hurting
Wandering but not lost
Shamed but not shameful
Violated but not broken
Broken, but whole

The fire in my soul
Thu, 29 Oct 2020

The fire in my soul

It might be dimmed

But it crackles

The music in my heart

It might be hushed

But it hums

The light in my eyes

It might be shadowed

But it simmers

The make of my armor

It might be broken

But I radiate through

For that is how I am made

Persistent

Resilient

Imperfectly Gloriously Perfect!

~ ✦ ~

Emerge

Wed, 23 Dec 2020

What is the invitation calling for

To Emerge

In my Glory

With my Light

With my Voice

What is the invitation into

To Immerse

Into my Divinity

Into my Shine

Into my Depths

What is to come

To Become

What I AM

And Soar

Emerge and Soar

UnBecome

Sun, 24 Jan 2021

UnBecome

The good girl

The adjusting wife

The dedicated mother

UnBecome

The beautiful girl

The elegant lady

The youthful elderly

UnBecome

The demure perfection

The subservient ambition

The unquestioning compliance

UnBecome

All that is taught

And

Become Unapologetic

Unconstrained

Unlimited YOU

UnBecome all

To Become YOU

What limiting beliefs are going to UnBecome?

~ ✦ ~

The Newness
Sat, 24 Apr 2021

Fresh and dewy

Glistening my song

Like raindrops

Dancing along

The joy

Seeping in Slowly making home

Making my heart roam

The rapture of hope

Filling my depths

Breaching through my crevices

Making me hum

And then some

The newness

Fresh and dewy.

~ ✦ ~

To love deeply and profoundly

Tue, 01 Jun 2021

To love deeply and profoundly

Is our divine nature

One we have UnBecome,

overshadowed by our conditioned self

So, what is awakening

It is Unlearning

Unraveling

UnBecoming

And coming back to our light

To the core essence of who we are

Unabashedly

Unapologetically

Free to Be

Step into it
Mon, 14 Jun 2021

Step into it with me Wholly

Fully

And Unrestrained.

Experience it

With your aura,

In your being.

If my spirit does not wake you, arouse you

Then I am not for you

If my mind does not

make you go deeper into your crevices

Then don't have me in there.

If my passion does not consume you

Wholly

And Fully

Then let me go and fill it with another presence.

For I want to

experience it all

with abandon

Wholly

Fully

And Unrestrained.

~ ✦ ~

From Transactional to Transcendental Love

Mon, 21 Jun 2021

Wholeness and unabashed acceptance of self

all of who we are

the beautiful and the ugly

the healed and the hurting

the luminous light and the engulfing darkness

All if it

A fulfilling communion with self to be whole in a communion

with another . . .

Is the journey of shifting from

transactional to

transcendental love

~ ✦ ~

Manifesting desires
Sun, 27 Jun 2021

Manifesting Companionship be like . . .
Laughing uncontrollably in Shared humor
Being lost in Meaningful conversations
Being secure in Unquestioned trust
Being sated in Great fucking sex
Exploring them Travel goals
Deep knowing in Mutual respect
And allowing the Space for growth
Not wanting to be made whole
But basking in each other's wholeness
Manifesting Companionship be like
. . . coming back home!

Courage
Thu, 29 Jul 2021

Courage

What does it look like

Silent

Stubborn

Resilient

Defiant

Standing behind that

smile Nestled deep in the

gaze of those eyes

It knows its essence

It holds its presence It cements its hold

amidst the chaos

And whispers

I see you

I know you

And you will come through.

Want to know what Courage looks like?

Peek within

And see your vibrant flame.

It is yours to claim!

~ ✦ ~

These little dew drops of love
Sat, 31 Jul 2021

These little drew drops of love

That clung behind

Hiding in the crevices of my heart.

They swelled

With hope

And affection

And passion for life.

Into a river

Flowing through me

In abandon.

Rushing to meet the ocean

And dissipating into

The vastness of me.

These little dew drops that stayed behind

Fill my being.

They gush out of me

In ecstasy of knowingness

That I am coming back home

To Me!

I am neither This nor That

Mon, 02 Aug 2021

I am This and That

and

all that is in between.

I am a flow of

contradictions

Blindingly luminous and

intensely dark.

Soft and sharp at edges

and in between.

Naively trusting and

guardedly closed.

Spiritually elevated and

unabashedly vain.

Unapologetically wild

and seemingly holy.

I don't fit in that box or

carry this label

I joyfully flow in my contradictions.

~ ✦ ~

I don't want to have lived
Tue, 03 Aug 2021

I don't want to have lived,

I want to have been alive.

I want to have mattered.

I want to have created a legacy.

For me, for those before me and ones that come after me.

One that unabashedly owns the living, the loving, the losing and the becoming.

One that celebrates the possibilities, the chasing, the falling and the making.

One that hums her music, even in the chaos of their noise.

One that knows to find herself, even in the mayhem of being everyone else.

I want to have been limitless,

In my potential and my pursuit.

I want to have basked in the light of those that I salute.

I want to have ignited that fire in those that I include.

I want to have known love, been in love, consumed by love and become love.

I want to have flowed gloriously in my contradictions and my imperfectly perfect trepidations.

I want to have embraced my shadows and become my light.

I don't want to have lived; I want to have been ALIVE!

The life that I make

Tue, 03 Aug 2021

There is a life we are

born into,

A life that we learn

to chase,

And then there is a life

we KNOW we are

meant for

THAT is the life I make.

~ ✦ ~

My first love
Tue, 17 Aug 2021

My love

. . . Words

I play with them

Chase them

Fondle them

Claim them mine

My intrigue

. . . Unbridled passion

I court it

Consume it Pour it – into the very

fiber of my being

My yearning

. . . Unabashed Living

I sing to it in my being

I caress it in my dream

And I taste it in my soul

What is yours?

Manifesting the love, I crave

Thu, 26 Aug 2021

Manifesting the love I

Crave

Be like

Dreamy

Scary

Intoxicating Assuring

Consuming

Filling

Arousing Awakening

Humbling Grounding Gratifying Knowing

Manifesting the love, I crave

Be like

Coming Home . . . to Me

It left me

Sun, 20 Feb 2022

Like the tale of two halves, it left me

Befuddled

Yearning

Wanting

Hurting

Doubting

Knowing

Realizing

Embracing

Laughing

Crying

Drowning in the deafening silence of my broken heart

And yet I rejoice in the thrill of having fallen freely, unconditionally, unapologetically and unabashedly in love with me

~ ~

I might not be your cup of tea
Tue, 01 Mar 2022

I might not be your cup of tea

But I'll be your shot of Whiskey

I'll burn down the branches of your chest as you breathe

Quenching the yearn that claims your insides

I'll fill you up with ecstasy

That will tether you at your limits

Inviting you to surrender to pleasure that scares the timid

I'll be this and all of the forbidden that

If you give me that unbridled darkness that is deep in there intact

I will not be your fucking sweet cup of tea

Cause I am that shot of whiskey

That cried tears as rapids down your cheeks

~ ✦ ~

Oh wait
Thu, 31 Mar 2022

Oh wait

I was gonna don that cloak of pessimism . . . for my wings of
optimism feel damp

But then this eerie, scintillating gush is playing with those feathers

Tingling, enticing and making me wonder

What if every moment of past has been so the present can be

What if we manifest every hidden desire to become the unbridled full
expression

As I hold on to my safe should

I ponder

The unmistakable thrill of unshackled free fall

What am I playing at?

~ ✦ ~

An ode to free fall
Tue, 12 Apr 2022

Those guttural moans bathed in pleasure

Singing to your throbbing heart

Luring you with my willingness into your sacredness

I ask of you

To love in abandon

To invite me into your allness

To allow me to give you my fears, my shame

In exchange of basking in the scent of us

In exchange of meeting, you where no-one ever has

My sacred essence and your prowess . . . They tangle

They tangle dancing to our lust, pulsating to our cravings

I crave you invading my warmth

Take me to my edges and then tipping over to oblivion

Those guttural moans

Giving an ode to our pleasure

They remind me of our cosmic dance

I welcome your love in my divine.

~ ✦ ~

I am

Mon, 18 Jul 2022

Tiny little specks of lights
That seep into my cracks
Filling me up with clarity
With knowing
Grounding me into my being
That I am becoming all that I desired
I am manifesting all that I aspire to experience
That I am, returning home to me!

~ ~

I still
Mon, 25 Jul 2022

I still share

The tug to her womb

The darkness of her silence

The blinding glare of her light

I still live in the comfort of her shadows

Peeking out to chase my light

I still breathe in

Her courage

Her resilience

Her valorous sacrifices

I still relish the dance of

Daughter, she raised

And the woman I have Become

~ ✦ ~

Old and familiar
Sat, 03 Sept 2022

This old and familiar

Trail of nostalgic ruins

That I end up at

Remind me what I can leave behind and co create anew

These old and familiar Ways to be that I fall into

Remind me

What I can grow out of and become with grace

These old and familiar crevices in my heart remind me

That my potential to manifest is boundless and Limitless

These old and familiar paths

Nudge me to birth anew

So on from old and familiar to old and familiar but New

~ ✦ ~

You are the Universe and She is You
Sat, 10 Sept 2022

For You, my love, are the universe and She is You

Limitless abyss of Mysteries held in her eyes

Miracles in her womb

Creation in her yoni

And the entangled embrace of light and darkness in her arms

She embraces you

Mesmerizing and tantalizing with her depth

Her unknown expressions waiting to be known

She births

She manifests

She creates

And she destroys

My love, that cosmic dance of Universe

And You Brought me to you

To Be

To Become The rapture of abandon in love

I asked the universe

Sat, 17 Sept 2022

I asked the universe

OK I am ready

I'm ready to step into my power to be my light and to love my shadows.

I thought it was a courageous, glorious declaration . . . ha-ha! and maybe it was.

I heard back – OK love!! And are you ready to do the work then?

I asked oh what would that be? Because aren't I already everything I want to be?

It answered yes you are! And you have to become what you are! You asked to come home – so walk the path, love!

Loudly and proudly ask for what you want to manifest but responsibility to co-create is yours.

Loudly and proudly asked to step into the vibration of your highest good. But the discipline of letting go of all that is not aligned is yours.

Loudly and proudly claim the joy, the pure love, the unbridled wonder every moment is.

But the responsibility to be in the moment, to embrace it with a wonder and curiosity, not preconditioned expectations, is yours.

Oh, I get it – I chose to come back home to me but the responsibility to walk the path is mine.

Haha – shit! cannot hide behind deflection or let the grace drop in my lap!

Gotta to do the work – carpola

Allowing

Sat, 24 Sept 2022

Allowing Abundance

Is such a tantric dance

Of attracting and letting go

Of manifesting and releasing

Of discerning and taking a leap of faith

Seeing abundance in experiences, in joy, in giving, in receiving

Accumulating wealth of abundant friendships, of possessions, of experiences that make me come alive

Brought me to face to face with my deepest resistance of letting go

Of shedding what does not align

Of releasing what does not calibrate any more

It brought me to the awareness that the biggest hurdle to me stepping into my abundant power

Was My Own Fear WHAT IF I BECOME ALL THAT I AM

The juxtaposition of my contradictions

The abysmal depths of my Compassion and fierceness of the Kali in Me

The child like joy I emanate and the brooding introversions I fiercely protect

The vanity I lovingly stroke and detached yogini that dances in my soul

Allowing abundance Is making it abundantly clear

That the unbecoming invites the abundance of Being

~ ✦ ~

Highest expression of myself
Mon, 7 Oct 2022

Disruptor. Innovator. Change agent

Being the highest expression of myself – What does it look like?

I am a juxtaposition of an abyss of empathy

And a ferocious fire of justice

I am fearless, limitless in my expressions

I love with abandon

I protect my loves like Kali

I chase my wildest desires with the gusto of a relentless tsunami

I fail, I fail often, and I always learn

I fall and I rise again and again

I own all of me

My luminescent light

My consuming shadows

I own all of my space

I marvel in it

I don't ask I step in

I am on a relentless pursuit of not just having lived But being alive

Seeing the edges of my limits and then expanding them beyond

I am constantly disrupting as-is to create the possibilities of anew

I am changing, I am UnBecoming and I am becoming all at once

All in service to my Being The highest expression of myself – what does it look like?

It looks like YOU – your unbridled, unlimited, unabashedly luminant being

Come – Let's Be

~ ✦ ~

Fuck fuck fuckety fuck

Tues, 18 Oct 2022

Oh, I wanted to Matter

To be purposeful

To be ambitious

To be relevant

I wanted to Effectuate change . . . In others 😊

Oh, The grandiose plans I allocated to my purpose of work, of living, of meaning of my existence

In motherhood In career In my seva

FUCK! So self-serving, so aggrandizing and so childishly naive

Oh, I wanted to be in love

I have been in love

I have chased love

I have been consumed by love

And I have grown out of love

Only to come down to FUCK I just want to be LOVE

Fuck fuck fuckety Fuck!

I have chased and strived and hustled to Become

Only to come back home To the crux of purpose of becoming Its to be alive – not living

To be present To be courageously authentically present In every moment

For it was never about the WHAT I did but HOW I lived

So, my purpose of work, is to show up with curiosity and wonder

~ ✦ ~

Her Light
Wed, 19 Oct 2022

ROAR she was called to, but she whispered, whimpered

SHINE she was meant to, but she tethered in shadows
LOVE unabashedly she wanted to, yet she shrunk herself to her fears
AWOKE her spirit was, but she clung to the darkness
To LET GO she desired, yet she already was
ANEW, BLOSSOMING, BEAMING, BECOMING

The Love she was

The Adoration she was seeking
The Light she was
The Luminance she was seeking
So, she left behind the Wanting, Desiring, Asking
And CLAIMED
The Love she is.

So there Universe!
Now YOU do your dance.
For SHE has made her move,

For SHE is claiming

HER LIGHT.

~ ✦ ~

I am Alive

Fri, 21 Oct 2022

I have not just lived

I AM alive.

I have mattered.

I have created a legacy.

For me, for those before me and ones that come after me.

One that unabashedly owns the living, the loving, the losing and the becoming.

One that celebrates the possibilities, the chasing, the falling and the making.

One that hums her music, even in the chaos of their noise.

One that knows to find herself, even in the mayhem of being everyone else.

I AM limitless, In my potential and my pursuit.

I have basked in the light of those that I salute.

I have ignited that fire in those that I include.

I have known love, been in love, consumed by love and become love.

I have flowed gloriously in my contradictions and my imperfectly perfect trepidations.

I have embraced my shadows and become my light.

I have not just lived,

I AM ALIVE!

~ ✦ ~

Coming home
Fri, 04 Nov 2022

And then I came home . . . to me

Leaving behind the hustle to become

Shedding the cloaks of acceptance

Stripping down to my truth

I sat naked and raw

Bathing in the courage of those that traversed before me

Humming their songs

Letting them bathe me in the river they dance in

Running their wrinkled, cracked fingers through my hair

Caressing my belly they said Darlin' now u get to make music that is yours

Now you get to live out aloud the seductive dance of your juxtapositions

Now that you are home my love

You can be the wild, untamed expression of your restless blood.

You are Home!

Epilogue

~ ✦ ~

That incessant Need to be Needed

Echoes rise from my soul, urging me to release the old.

Cataclysms swell within and threaten to split me open.

I breathe.

I release.

I return – to the brittle comfort of what I already know.

Old patterns linger nudging me to shape into the vessel I am poured
into.

I should be a river – my own raging current, my own edge – and yet I
do not know how to emerge.

A storm of grief and sorrow brews, mourning a death I never named.

I kneel and ask the universe

Teach me to fill myself – with ME, and with the vastness of YOU.

Show me how to live in my home with ME

~ ✦ ~

www.ingramcontent.com/pod-product-compliance
Lightning Source LLC
Chambersburg PA
CBHW021205130626
46554CB00005B/1995